The Silent After

By

L.C. Stuart

ISBN: 1-4107-8826-1 (e-book)
ISBN: 1-4107-8825-3 (Paperback)

This book is printed on acid free paper.

1stBooks - rev. 01/12/04

I give my thanks to Jesus
for making the impossible, possible.

I dedicate this book to my husband Ivan,
daughter Shelida Natasha-Ann, and cousin Clara Sutton.

Contents

This Pain Called Hurt

Here I am I have this pain,
The feeling I can't explain.
Once I was a rich man,
With everything in the palm of my hand.

Along came hurt,
Treating me like dirt.
Everywhere I turned,
There was nothing in return.

Doctors can't cure this pain.
Rivers of tears driving me insane.
Emotions stabbing me in the heart,
So strong it's tearing me apart.

This pain called hurt,
I can't run or hide,
It'll be there whenever I arrive.

The Unforgettable Love

We come into this world
Looking for love.
A strong cry that's very well heard,
Just waiting to be hugged.

From that day on,
We never want to be alone.
Just a touch means so much,
Someone waiting to love us without a search.

That first attraction to a friend,
Love is there never wanting it to end.
Love is a beautiful feeling.
Love is in our heart, even when we're ill.

When we feel nobody loves us,
Remember the greatest love of all—
The love of Jesus,
The son of God.
That love will never wear off.

Coming from above,
The Unforgettable Love.

Less Than a Mile

God gave me courage,
Without a worry.
There was once a time,
Jesus wasn't on my mind.

A change in my life style,
Was less than a mile.
Darkness in my house,
As quiet as a mouse.

Only one income coming in,
Dear God, there's no end.

Give and it shall be given unto you,
This life style just won't do.
God is by your side,
Pray, God won't leave you behind.

Jesus Is

Jesus is the sun,
That brings us daylight,
Everyday of our life.
Without the sun,
We couldn't see
The beautiful flowers that bloom.

Jesus is the darkness,
That reminds us of the shining stars,
Against the dark blue sky.
Without the darkness bringing night,
No peaceful sleep; nothing goes right.

Jesus is the rain,
That makes the grass grow in the spring,
Without the rain pouring on the earth,
There will be no water to quench our thirst.

Jesus is alive today, in every way.
Put your trust in Him,
He will forgive you for all your sins.

Walking with Jesus

Passing through this life we're in,
We need to walk with Jesus
Until the end.

In a time of anger,
Stop and listen to yourself.
You're walking with Jesus now;
That anger can turn into happiness.

In a time of trouble,
You feels no one loves you.
You're walking with Jesus now,
He's your protector.

The best friend you ever had,
Turns his back on you.
You're walking with Jesus now,
There's love in your heart
For that friend too.

In a time of death,
We don't know what to do.
Turn to Jesus and say,
With you Jesus, I will make it through.

When men put you down,
Remember...
Jesus Christ is still around.

In the Beginning 1991

In the beginning 1991
Whoever thought they would be the one?
I wish it was only a dream,
The date January fifteenth.

That sound ringing in my ear.
Is it time to celebrate?
Is it time to cry?
Is it time to die?

The night before the count down,
Silent, silent all around.
The night after,
Tears, tears, no laughter.

TV's and radio's played the same tune,
War, War with a big boom.
The nightmare wasn't Halloween,
The date January fifteenth.

In the beginning 1991,
The end, we don't know.
Hope and all prayers,
Leads us not into despair.

O, Peace Where Can You Be?

Yesterday peace had no sound.
Today, it's no where to be found.
Drop everything today.
Tomorrow you're on your way.

O, peace where can you be?
All the ships on the sea
Looking for peace.
Oh where can you be?

All the jets in the sky,
Flying way up high,
Looking down and all around,
O, peace where can you be?
Each teardrop from the eye,
Meaning we don't like to say good-bye.

Remembering you in our prayers,
God knows we really do care.
Deep in our heart
We're never apart.

Why, we might not understand,
This day was already planned.
God is watching over you,
Don't forget, no matter what you do.

Dear Angel

Dear Angel: spread your wings.
Provide a shelter
That no man can explain.

Say it over and over again,
What a great country we're in.
Without all the brave men,
And all the brave women,
We have no power within.

Whether it's air or ground.
War is at us from every angle.
You can hear the sounds
Like echoes; voices singing.

War, War please no more.
The cry goes on—
Americans, American, American,
Please come back home.

Thoughts...Oh, Never Mind

While sitting on my bed,
All thoughts
Going through my head.
I wonder how many are dead.
That thought crosses my mind,
Then I say, "Oh, never mind."

While sitting on my bed,
I wonder about
The days over there.
That thought crosses my mind,
Then I say, "Oh, never mind."

While sitting on my bed,
I wonder about
The bombs instead.
That thought crosses my mind,
Then I say, "Oh, never mind."

All thoughts are real;
People are being killed.
On my knees I pray:
God show us a better day.

In My Dreams

Wherever you might be
I can't see you,
But I believe you see me.
What you said has come true.

I know you heard the cry,
"I love you, I love you,
Please, don't say good-bye."
I'll never forget, no matter what I do.

All the things I took for granted.
If I had one more chance.
You'll seem as one big planet.
I'll realize the greatness with a glance.

Your hair, eyes, and nose,
Oh, how I wish I could see,
Your whole body and soul.
How great that would be!

The sound of your voice,
The touch of your hands,
Life without you wasn't my choice.
Maybe one day I will see you again.

I never realized;
There's no one on earth like you.
A love full of smiles,
That lift me up when I am blue.

Alone
in my home,
What you said
has come true—
"You're gonna
miss me

When I'm
dead and gone."

This
is not a song.

I miss you.
In my heart
and my dreams,
You're not gone.

Country

Along this narrow road,
I will travel.
Over the hills,
Around the curves,
Across the bridges I will go.

There's nothing to fear.
Just the smell
Of plums in the air.
Such a relaxing feeling;
Green pastures as far as I can see.

I travel this old road by night,
Such a long, dark road.
Quiet, and no one in sight.
Only the deer are so bold.

The sound of crickets
In the bush just a foot away.
Oh country, I'm glad you're around;
I'm no longer feeling down.

Life with Winter, Spring, Summer. Fall

Come with me we're going for a walk.
You can make it long or short;
We'll make the decision as we talk.
Life on this road can be cold or hot.

How about a walk through winter?
Life here is too cold.
This journey needs something warm and tender,
A little love to warm the soul.

Now we're going through spring.
Life seems to be just right.
Love and happiness come with the rain.
Everything seems so sweet and nice.

Here we go passing through summer;
Life is so hot and dry.
It's too hot. But remember,
You can make it if you try.

Well, here we go with fall.
Life is cooling down just a little.
Watch out! You think you have it all,
But you're only in the middle.

Finally here's that fork in the road;
Which way shall we go?
Easy now, don't be so bold,
Make up your mind-
before it's too late.

I Work for America

Some people look at me
with a frown.
If it wasn't for hard work,
I wouldn't be around.

Easy work and soft hands
Isn't my plan.
Rough hands and strong muscles—
That's my hustler.

Eight hours in the sun,
I can stand it with a burn.
Eight hours in the cold,
To me that's a pot of gold.

I'm as happy as I can be.
Because I work
to make America better,
For you and me.

What a Man

I'm Proud to say, "What a man."
He works his fingers to the bone.
I love looking at those strong hands.
Here he comes, can't wait to get home.

That nine to five just won't do.
Eight hours just won't pay.
Twelve hours just to pay the bills that are due.
Hard work he'll take any day.

He doesn't mind working up a sweat.
Not enough white shirts in his field.
Sweat shirts, "Yes, you bet."
Greasy hands is all in the deal.

No time for personal phone calls.
Thirty minutes for a sack lunch;
Back to work and on the ball.
He's the greatest of them all!

His week comes to an end.
No going out tonight.
Just time with family and maybe a friend.
Now he can sit down and take a bite.

Give Me a Chance

Five days a week I work;
This isn't my life I pray.
Circumstances in my way.
I need to see a better day.

This old job I shall quit;
They're treating me like a witch.
I can survive without the benefits.
No more games, no more tricks.

How nice it feels,
Having a relaxed mind.
No more nine to five.
Relax today, tomorrow I'll look.

That voice ringing in my ear,
"We'll keep your app. on file.
You are qualified,
But right now we're not hiring."

Unemployment line,
You're not leaving me behind.
Someone, somewhere
Will give me a chance.
Because, I need a job
To help with my finances.

Just One More Bite

On this lake I will stand;
All the fish at my hand.
Cast out, reel in,
I'll catch it
Before you count to ten.

Come on! Come on!
Just one more bite.
The sun going down;
Soon it will be night.

Five, ten, fifteen, twenty—
I'm not disappointed.
Relax, count to ten.
God will bless you
Again and again.

Crack, Crack, Who's There?

Crack, crack, who's there?
Give me a rock;
I don't care.

The Lord is knocking at your door.
Confess in him,
He's all your needs
And more.

Your cup is running over.
Look at the world you're in.
Wake up brother; get sober.
This world is coming to an end.

Your family is first in your life,
'Til death do you part.
Put drugs out and you will see the light.
Right now crack, not Jesus, is in your heart.

Pray. The Lord wants you to open the door.
Jesus is knocking; it's not too late.
Please open the door for God's sake.
Before your world comes to an end.

Sex the Killer

Just one time,
Might be a crime.
I can't decide;
Will I do it or will I…

Oh! That killing disease,
Won't put my mind at ease.
This one time
Might be the death of me.

A nightmare I'll never forget,
Because I got rid of it.
That crime—
Always on my mind.

Sex can kill.
And God forgives.
It's sex the killer.
Stay safe—
Do it God's way.

A Prayer for Better Health

Dear God, I need to better my health,
More than I need wealth.
Medical problems in my way.
Medication keeping me alive day by day.

Cholesterol clogging my veins.
Dear God,
I've used food in vain.
For me there will be no heart attack.
Starting today I will fight back.

Man can't live by bread alone.
Vegetables, chicken and fish won't hurt a bone.
Eight or more glasses of water a day is my need.
God will give me fresh air to breathe.
This diet doesn't cost a dime.
O God, what peace of mind.

One day I'll look back
And wonder:
O God, what happen to all that fat?
God as I pray,
Give me faith to live every day.
God this is how I feel.
Only *you* have the power to heal.
Amen! Amen!

Twenty-Nine

Age has a number,
Depending on what you can remember.
Right now is the borderline;
I am now twenty-nine.

Feel like the good times are running out.
Maybe thirty is what it's all about.
Wait just a minute, twenty-nine!
There's a lot more planning on my mind.

No! No! No!

Here it is, that big three-O.
I might be thirty; I don't know.
All those numbers aren't too bad.
This feeling is the best I ever had.

I might skip right on through to sixty.
I've never felt so beautifully.
Watch out thirty, forty, fifty.
I'm smarter, and in heart richer.

Just remember,
Age is only a number.
Maybe eighty
Is the greatest.

Right now twenty-nine,
You're out of my mind.

Tears Don't Make Me Cry

We're crying out,
In this world everywhere.
A mind controlled by endless doubt,
Makes me wonder who cares.

The weather man is saying
It's going to be twenty below.
I'm praying
Give me shelter or give me cover.

As I walk along this street,
Please don't pass me by.
I'll work for something to eat.
Please tears, don't make me cry.

People just don't understand.
How did this happen to me?
I once had it all in my hands.
Maybe tomorrow I'll be off the street.

One Plus One Equals Two Faces

Stay away from the smiling faces;
Getting help from them ends in disgrace.
They'll stab you in the back
With that grin so big and fat.

When you're down
They will stomp you in the ground.
When you're up they'll look at you with a frown.
The two faces will always be around.

Keep on gossiping,
But watch what you say.
Someone else is watching you daily.
Stay away from me;
Your comments I don't need.

I've got Him on my side.
He has given me all the pride.
I know what has been said about me.
Two faces, two faces you just can't see.

Smile, smile, smile.
But this time
Make it last a while.
One plus one equals two faces.

Memories—Where Can Daddy Be?

Dear Dad,
The year 1952—
That wasn't a year to be sad.
You were happy then; now I am too.

There's a tall, handsome man;
He's watching me.
Why? I can't understand.
Maybe South Carolina isn't the place to be.

Hey pretty little lady,
May I ask your name?
Believe me, I'm not crazy.
And I don't believe in playing games.

He's too nice to be real.
Tell me, what can I do?
He's controlling the way I feel.

My friend told me about him today;
There's another lady in his life.
Being a Georgia Girl what can I say.
Life isn't guaranteed to always be nice.

I'm happy now; I met his sister.
She is just as nice
And a good listener too.

In a few days I'll be leaving S.C. behind.
Leaving those good old dreams.
Oh Georgia, you're always on my mind.
S.C. was only a dream.

I'll visit our meeting place one more time.
I'm leaving dear ol' James behind.

The year 1953—
I thought it was only a dream.
Now I'm wondering what will it be.
The day's are getting longer it seems.

By the way, it's a girl you see.
Dear James, I may never see you again.
She is eighteen now; wondering where can daddy be.

I've got two boys now.
Supporting three kids isn't easy;
There's no daddy for them.
They're asking, where can Daddy be?

Tell Me, What Do You See?

Tell me, tell me,
What do you see?
Lights, lights on a Christmas tree.
As pretty as pretty can be.

Tell me, tell me,
What do you see?
Something white as white can be.
Looks like snow to me,
All on a Christmas tree.

Tell me, tell me,
What do you see?
Gifts, gifts, gifts,
Wrapped so beautifully.

Tell me, tell me,
What do you see?
Children, children, children,
As happy as happy can be.

Tell me, tell me,
What do you see?
Kids, kids, that worries me.
Why can't they be
As happy as happy can be?

Tell me, tell me,
What do you see?
Angels, Angels, Angels,
Bringing love, joy and gifts
To the kids that concern me.

Tell me, tell me,
What do you see?

Colors:
Red, Yellow, Black and White.
Jesus loves you.
We're all his children
believing in reality.

Tell me, tell me,
What do you see?
A cheerful face looking at me.

Smile, smile, smile,
It's Jesus that you see.

This Is My Home

Jesus cares for me.
Otherwise, where would I be?
Family and friends I might not see.
But Jesus has provided this home
Just for me.

Nurses watch over me day by day.
Thank you Jesus. Thank you Jesus as I pray.
People see me and say,
I'm just old and gray.

God looks down at me and says,
I'm with you all the way.
Take this home as a gift,
There's more blessings
To bless you with.

For me this is just the beginning.
This is a peaceful living.
God has delivered me from sin;
For me there's no end.

The Silent Cry

The silent cry
You can hear.
Deep dark secrets,
Reminding you of the old days.

Stand up! Stand up! Be counted.
Looking back where the sun sets—
The two-room shack
With the kerosene lamps.

Sitting by the fireplace,
Breakfast cooking
On a wood stove.
Kids hating to go out in the cold.

That three mile walk to school
Was more than a thought.
Remembering those blizzard days,
Strong winds cutting you in the face.

Two mile walk to a movie
On a sunny day.
Forty cent is what you pay;
Away to the balcony.

The dark dirt road
With the church on the hill,
Deep in the valley
While the creek flows water—
A mother holds her child's hand.
Then the sound of car tires
Roaring on the road.

The silent cry had no tears to dry.
The silent cry will never say good-bye.

Just a Baby

I'm just a baby you see.
Without me,
Where would mommy be?

I love her and she loves me.
Without mommy,
Where would I be?

I cry day and night.
But mommy tells me,
"Baby, everything's all right."
If I could put it all together
Things would be so much better.

Why? I can't say the words.
Mommy looks me in the eyes,
And they're very well heard.

I love you, Mom.
You're the greatest!
And I'm number one.

A Mother's Love

Mother, this praise
Is for you,
For making my life
A living truth.
Because there's nothing
In this world
More precious than
A mother's love.

I give my thanks to Jesus
For watching over you.
All the blessings
Without reasons.

I can't explain the feeling
In my heart.
But something deep down inside
Is saying
Mother, we'll never be apart.

My School

I'm so proud of my school.
My teacher taught me all the rules.
I have a teacher so great,
She's always early, never late.

I learned my ABC's.
I can count way past one, two, three.
I love my school;
There's always something to do.

I love to run and play.
Most of all my teacher makes my day.
You must remember this and that.
While Jack keeps hitting me in my back.

One, Two, Three, ABC

One, two, three,
ABC,
Jesus loves me.
Oh where would I be?

It's easy to say
"Oh, they're just little kids."
But my thoughts are big, big, *big*.

One, two, three,
ABC,
I'm as happy as I can be.

Planet Earth

God created the planet Earth,
Within it, air to breathe.
God created the sun,
The birds, the flowers and the trees.

God created the rivers,
The ocean and the sea.
God created you
And God created me.

Greater Is He

He's brave; he's strong.
He makes our house a home.
He's a worker,
My bread, my maker.

His deep sounding voice
Touches my heart.
He's my Father.
Most of all he's my star.

He's powerful; he's wonderful.
He leadeth me without a sorrow.
Greater is he—
That's a Father to me.

Merry Christmas, Mom and Dad

Merry, Merry Christmas, Mom.
I'm praising you
For all the good things you've done.
You make my world a pleasure.

Merry, Merry Christmas, Dad.
I'm praising you.
Without you what would I have had?
You're everything I believe in too.

I give my thanks to Jesus
For watching over you.
All the blessings out of no reason.
Without Jesus what would I do?

Honor thy Mother and thy Father.
I say this from the deepest of my heart.
Without you life would be harder.
I love you, I love you Mom and Dad.

Dear Jesus

There are times
When I am confused.
I don't know what to do;
I wonder who can I turn to.

I begin to cry out
Lord Jesus Christ,
What am I going to do?

Dear Jesus,
Make my good dreams come true.
Because Lord
I do believe in you.

Jesus Has Got a Blessing for Me

Jesus has got a blessing for me.
He's got me on this highway, you see.
There's no traffic to stop me;
The light is always green.

Jesus has got a blessing for me.
I don't have to wait;
There's no yellow light on this street.
Keep on going, keep on going.

Jesus is telling me,
Don't you stop, don't you stop.
There's no red light on this street.
Keep on going, keep on going.

He filled me up with his own gas;
There's no running out on this street.
Keep on going, keep on going.
Jesus has got a blessing for me
And Jesus got a blessing for you.

Come Let's Join Together

Let us speak the words
From the most high above.
Come let us join together,
Words of peace for one another.

We have the eyes to see
That all men want to be free.
A voice to sing out,
Hallelujah, Hallelujah, Hallelujah.

We have the ears to hear
The voices crying out.
We in America want our people free.
Come join together
All the hands in this nation,
Feel the power of freedom
Forcing its way home.

Don't Point the Finger at Me

For all the drugs
Being abused in the world—
Stop!
Don't point the finger at me.

All the killing you see
On T.V.—
Stop!
Don't point the finger at me.

The robbery
of a nearby store—
Stop!
Don't point the finger at me.

All the illegitimate babies,
Mothers on welfare—
Stop!
Don't point the finger at me.

I'm not what you hear;
I am love, understanding,
And peace.

That's when you point
The finger at me.

I Saw You Standing There

Why is it a dream?
Maybe in my sleep
I was taken away
Along with another human being.

I saw you standing there
Waiting to be recognized.
I looked you in the eyes.
You began to speak
The words I couldn't hear.

Don't Be a Quitter

Go to school.
Follow the rules.
Learn all that you can.
Now say it again.

Don't be a quitter.
As you get bigger
You'll understand.
No education—
Your life could be
in someone else's hand.

The Silent After

The mind of every human being
Experiences the Silent After.
Many words unspoken
That only you can hear.

That great *inside* in control
Talking to you,
Telling you what to do.
Listen, listen now!

It lives within you—
The Silent After,
Giving you the break
To wonder away.

The Savior

Say to the world,
God has given me faith.
Lift up your arms;
Talk to the most high above.

Believe in your heart
That He's a powerful God.
He's our creator.
Above all He's our savior.

Drugs Lead You by the Nose

Drugs are taking food from your family table.
Drugs take the life of your baby.
God knows,
Drugs lead you by the nose.

Drugs control the brain.
They are not always called cocaine.

You can fight back
With the help of Jesus;
That's a fact.

Easter Bunny

Easter Bunny, Easter Bunny,
What do you have?
Something sweet, sweeter than honey.

Easter Bunny, Easter Bunny,
What can you give?
Easter eggs, Easter eggs,
All in one bag,

Easter Bunny, Easter Bunny,
All Fluffy and white,
I have something too.
And it's all for you.
One yellow Easter egg,
Two chocolate bars—
My gift to you
From the bottom of my heart.

About the Author

L.C. started writing poetry just for herself in high school. She enjoyed very much reading the books of Psalms. She wrote maybe three or four poems within twenty years after High School. Not until 1990, she began to take writing a little more seriously, when some of her writing was being published in Anthologies. In August 1991, She was inducted into the International Society of Poets. L.C. and her family now live in Lithonia, Georgia.